I kinda used to think Death was a whole other different room, a foreign state without lungs or shape. You got into the elevator and the doors went ping, up all the floors, forever and ever. But then I read Damon Potter's incredible new collection of poems and I started to think, hm. Maybe not. Maybe death isn't capitalized, maybe it's a condition of a body rearranging itself, maybe it's just as political as presence, maybe you still have to cast a vote for the Idiot President no matter what, when, where, how. And then there's the thing about how these poems made me sadsmile all throughout (sometimes I sadchuckled!), and there was this aftertaste in my mouth I took with me everywhere among the living things.

RAUL RUIZ
Author of *Mustard* (Drop Leaf Press, 2022)

a signifier. a magnification of whiteness sullied through a soft reflective voice. previously butterflied, now brought to life, Damon Potter explores the crossroads of a hyperbolic existence into a cooing revelry of defiance and opposition. where most white writers, in their attempt to dissect their white colonial industrial complex, wreak havoc by imposing readers with their own self-obsession; Potter has carefully and gently, brought himself to the stand with the intention of self-awareness. awareness that permeates through meditation, through cognisance, through disruption, and through calling out (one's self and/or/for others who have also been indoctrinated). i want to un. claim. all of the times. i've ever said. they. that othering vein. hangry within me. this work is not a removal or disinheritance of whiteness, but instead a whisper of acknowledgement of one's inherited positionality. it screams; i see myself, what i am, and what i can become. its an incision against whiteness that gets it, and most essentially, gets it right.

MIMI TEMPESTT
Author of *the delicacy of embracing spirals* (City Lights, 2023)

SEEING and LOOKING

Cover photograph: Carolyn Ho
Cover art: Truong Tran
Cover and interior typeface: Futura, Helvetica, Georgia and Arial
Cover and interior design: Carolyn Ho

Library of Congress Cataloging-in-Publication Data

Names: Potter, Damon, 1985- Seeing and looking. | Tran, Truong, 1969-
Looking and seeing.
Title: Seeing and looking : poems, essays, fragments / Damon Michael Potter.
Looking and seeing : poems, essays, fragments / Truong Tran.
Other titles: Seeing and looking | Seeing and looking.
Description: Oakland, California : Omnidawn, 2023. | Two works bound
back-to-back and inverted; titles from separate title pages. | Summary:
"Looking And Seeing is a poetic work of equal parts yearning, regret and
righteous indignation. On these pages, what is said and what is written
renders us seen in all our complications. I wrote this book as a
singular and lifelong investigation of my being and my body as someone
brown moving through white spaces. That it now finds itself bound
together in a single volume and in proximity to the work of my friend
Damon Potter, that he is a white man and I am a brown man, and that I am
writing this into existence, means the world to me. Seeing and Looking
is a recording taken in proximity to my friend Truong Tran. In this
book, I examine who I am and who I want to be, the complications and
realities of trying to be good while also benefitting from our
oppressive past and present. I am oppressor. And also my friends die.
Someday I'll die. I witness horrible acts. I witness the moon. I
remember awful grains I've committed myself. In Seeing and Looking, I
wonder how to be respectfully dying while everyone else is also dying.
In Seeing and Looking, I witness my self"-- Provided by publisher.

Identifiers: LCCN 2023019350 | ISBN 9781632431233 (trade paperback)
Subjects: LCSH: American poetry--21st century. | Self--Poetry. |
Death--Poetry. | Autobiographical poetry, American. | LCGFT: Poetry.
Classification: LCC PS595.S43 L66 2023 | DDC 811/.6--dc23/eng/20230627
LC record available at https://lccn.loc.gov/2023019350

Published by Omnidawn Publishing, Oakland, California

www.omnidawn.com
10 9 8 7 6 5 4 3 2 1
ISBN: 978-1-63243-123-3

Poems • Essays • Fragments

SEEING
and
LOOKING

damon potter

OMNIDAWN • OAKLAND, CALIFORNIA • 2023

CONTENTS

i.

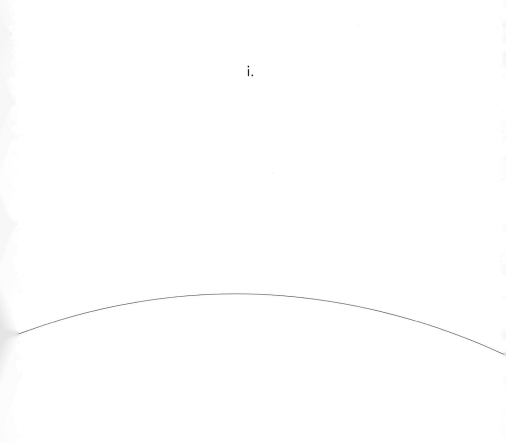

i think a lot how i couldve died
driving a fork lift
couldve smooshed others
with the forks high
pallets of hard things
heavy
or spikes
falling like humpbacks
falling like borders

death is unequal
and all of us die
the part thats unequal
is being alive
knowing the how
or why of your die
and how that why die
relates to a body

i wonder if ill die then bide
heaven up there
or in dirt
will i send myself to hell
for privileges
or for words
that did fall too
from a fruit tree

i will die
with tshirt on
made one day
in vietnam
i will die
with socks
and food
soiled jeans
and bedside
shoes
i will die
and so will you
well all die
from different views
dos
and donts
and poisons

i will die
im sliced up thighs
im a hambone
turkey
rye
im in berkeley
roast beef
bye

what is the joint
in writing a poem
people are dying
killed by the state
and i want to hug us
all before dying
i want to hug us
all before fate

like peppermint sticks
or silver york patties
its cold in my mouth
from all of the violence
cops have intent to kill
every black man
Latinos
some women
like just down the street
cops shot a kid
hidden by car lids
and in sacramento cops
shot a man named
Stephon Clark

i find that my mom and i dont collide much
when i am dry high and feeling fine
she is then sad
she has seen friends who are just dying
she tries to not say or tell me these things
she i think knows that i am a desert
and when i am feeling lay in bed rude
she has a hard time
accepting my rue and boney fingers
and i have a hard time
knowing shes dying how all people do
and i will miss her

when i die will i be dead
will i move on
from the language
i have said
that
i have said
that ive said

ill first die
and then ill find
im a fly
by grey cloud sky
or im summer
warm and thunder
billowed pillows
no im fall
plants fake dying
sun
im cold

death is a place
ill go to die
some of us dont go
some of us try
into that next life
this ones been good
ill see you later
some people limp there
like they are paper
peanuts for packing
leftover food
some people wait there
some people choose
some people sudden

connor is dead now
like a potato
he cannot fade though
he has my books
he has my books
i will forget them
but i love potatoes
and how they look

i will die
cuz im alive
and living
is too busy
i will die
cuz im alive
and living
is a frisbee

you are now sick
and they dont know
happens
they are there scanning
every pore downside
an orange leaf
they will conclude
what they always do
your body has fungus
eating clam chowder
i mean
your body has aphids
eating your flower

poems dont work when thinking ill health. im thinking of yours
bob i hope for your health.

my dad would drive us to a lake
lake hennessey specifically conn dam
when it was raining
so we could see water fall in a big hole.
i know my body will fall in a big hole
and thats the worst that will happen to me
oroville dam is leaking
its dead
theres water and algae
and someday my prostate
will squeeze all my limbs

when i die will i pretend
hacky sacked
or held my
breath
throw my billfold
from a ledge
and ill get up to get it
its money

we know folks
who are leaf backs
they are green
and decent ones
full of sap
and fast like limes
we all know some
pretty leaf backs
shiny folks
and then they die

when i die will i be left
as whales dead
floating
where the sand is wet
will they cut me up instead
of pushing me
to sea
will they look
and try to glean
the evidence
for things we see
each and every
sun warped day
all around us

death cooked grandma
while i worked
couldnt get there
cuz
well
work
my mom called
she cried and said
damon
sorry
grandmas
dead

and never did i see her again

death is rash like mustard greens
grazing like some cattle
death has often looked like me
and this i need to saddle

will i turn to stinky mush that feeds a bush
will a tiny insect
bug
pick me up
or lay an egg
in the sap
that once was leg
am i bratwurst
am i dead

i will die from eating stuff
candy
grapefruit
celery
fluff
i will die from right wing duff
dander gushed now like its slander
i will die from lies and bluffs
or the pandered
action of the fearful neighbor
huffing puff

will exhaust inside my chest
mingle with my stinky breath
will i cough up worms
and pets and donut
steps
with blood
unsaid
will i die like all
the dead
the yet to dead
in debt
til dead

if i die
before i wake
tell my neighbors
i have saved
rice
and squash
up on my shelf
they can have it
its all theirs

death is like when i eat lunch
cuz everything
that stuffs my guts
like peanut buttered
sandwich
bread
is made of people
dead

death is when i muse
at death
cuz im not dead
im a rug
and deaths a carpet
i just lay
on top of death
and cover death
like im reporters
i smother death
to dead

ii.

i want to un
claim
all of the times
ive ever said
they
that othering vein
hoarding within me

i want to un
claim
all of the times
ive ever said
they
that othering vein
hulking within me

i want to un
claim
all of the times
ive ever said
they
that othering vein
herding within me

i want to un
claim
all of the times
ive ever said
they
that othering vein
hoping within me

i want to un
claim
all of the times
ive ever said
they
that othering vein
hawking within me

i want to un
claim
all of the times
ive ever said
they
that othering vein
harbored within me

i want to un
claim
all of the times
ive ever said
they
that othering vein
hollow within me

i want to un
claim
all of the times
ive ever said
they
that othering vein
harrow within me

i want to un
claim
all of the times
ive ever said
they
that othering vein
hashbrowned within me

i want to un
claim
all of the times
ive ever said
they
that othering vein
haloed within me

i want to un
claim
all of the times
ive ever said
they
that othering vein
happy within me

i want to un
claim
all of the times
ive ever said
they
that othering vein
hammered within me

i want to run
claim
all of the times
ive ever said
they
that othering vein
hangry within me

i want to un
claim
all of the times
ive ever said
they
that othering vein
hurting within me

iii.

i should be more like a blackberry thing
pricking
aggressive the boorish
and mean
and holding my fruit out
to summer bowls:
this country is racist
and i receive clout
bodily safety
because i am white
white folks dont say it
we write our books
about what we pick up
or about fruit

cathy
if you say
again
my friends a burrito
i wont want to
be your friend

i dont know the words for me
ive said mean things
and still my body runs with need
to catch a tumbled orange

i am a string bean
tree trunk
a plate
and can i be better
once i am staked
something to hold me
lift me
like hey
or is it within me
to be a good thing
on my own

margarite
not sure why i passed my time
for asking you
what you asked me
you demonstrated
decency and me
well
we saw clear
im opponent
to the thoughtful.
dear

dont want the white world
to barber
protect me
from all the right words
that people
will tell me
about my racist
and privilege
my belt
i want to hear them
so that my self
can be more aware
and i can tell others
like i did yesterday

perhaps on a monday
all of us white folks
will forget
like some play doh
learned
or our trained
othering ways
well slant like tomatoes
walk
ride the bus
dance to some music
or watch the sun
and respect everyone

iv.

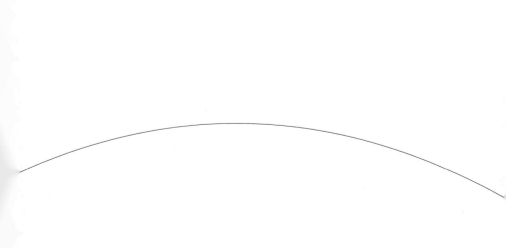

the people i work with they are amazing
they do put strangers
ahead of them
first
red to a purple
though im unsure what colors mean
the people i work with
are letters to words

dads a cop
he was a cop
he is a cop
its in his mud

i am a fresh yam
come from the ground
carried around
like im in a basket

i was once planted
and hope to get back there

maybe thats how
we learn behaviors
stack our logs up
but not like the neighbors do it
the methods need working
not like the tech guys
never for profit
just to be nicer
respect agency
and stop killing people

can i erect
from this plastic sheet
respect
dignity
for other people
or is it all fawn gone
spoked
like some antifreeze
poured on the ground

there are still folks
for whom the want
privacy
means a big coat
jacket or sheet
masturbate
eat
shit and or pee
read be or sleep
away from the people
under a coat

i wanna be filed
or excuse me on file
mp3 virus
one trojan horse
to type tap present
the self that i do want seen
so other people
and also the robots
know how i feel
even when what i think
to me isnt seen

please do jack
inside my breast
tickle
tinkle
hammer
quest
crack
my grown
unfeelingness
cuz i cant find it
touch you
this

im a blessed hand
in the park
scraping at the landscape
bark
looking for my parts
or rings
like a beep detector
keys
wrapped or dropped
plattered
pinged

i think of my securities
and paddle harder
pulling now
at living trees

surf
cordilleras
dead ones unfettered

among the red rabbits
jack rats and lizards
i am a live one
living in weather
parked in the pampas grass
down at big sur

im a peacock
im a dresser
getting soft
along the weather
cheesy plates
and sugar grapes
i know that i will die

im a gadget
twirled and stuffed
inside a packet
and when my habit
wants enough
it has it
and pulls me from the bin

when i die will i be skin
skinnier
still have my bed
will my body
upside down
around the town
or buried in the ground
be dressed

i of course wonder why all the people
pictured you hang up
photograph
nude
why theyre all white men
and more important
why i think you
saying why
yes
not every picture
is of whiteness

would you say that?

truong my reluctance
to say aloud thoughts
is a considerate
one in a bunch of dandelion pokers.
i want to be sure
that ive done my thinking
thought the abrades out
morning and noontime
perhaps on til rust or when the moons up.
id like for patience
to grow out a leaf cut
without the thorns
sprout my own worm head
turn a bright stem
then a puff
seed sent
into a brick to grow this mutation
of what whiteness trains.

i am a condo
moon
im a bimbo
i am a pinhole
camera
a bust
(as in failure)
i am the ginkgo up the street
block
wearing no gold now
the world is fucked up

i am an ignorant
spool
drool
im metal
chipped off the kettle
also im nice too
but neither matters
we are our bodies
which code how the words work
people perceive us
however theyre sure

i might be a camera
snuck
inside a theater
or i might not be

i am like that spackle stuff
popcorn
dust
up on the ceiling

im asbestos
anthrax
slime
im turpentine
and im bright like primer

when my apple cell phone
rings
everyone thinks
their phones ringing
and when another cell phone
rings
i think its my phone ringing

when my mom went into target
she didnt take too long
she bought a brand new coffee maker
sixty dollars
gone

v.

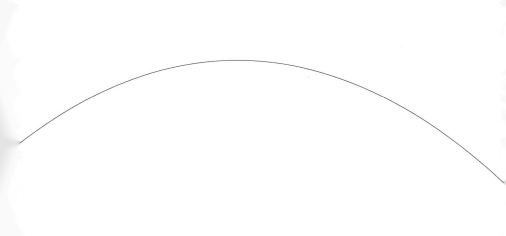

when i fruit
am i elastic
sappy glanced
and furred
with chances
cuz im white and male bodied?
can i prove
that im a basket
happy stanced
and pure as practice
despite my white and male body?

•

i will be gentle
see and respect
the worldy curled dimples
made by the wind
and battleship moments
i will attend to all of my training
listen and skip
while im celebrating
successes of other people

•

each of the moments in my work life
is a new chance for a tiger to bite me
on my insides
puddle me
striped
whirled on the floor
at someones resiliency
inside the gore of stigma

●

the only place i trust my words
is written
in this perm or bowl
written on an upside furl
cuz i have time to think
and twirl
the world that i would like

but this is outside life

●

when i am unsure
what to then say
i try to remember
to slow myself
down
remind myself
listen
no bead to talk
just be there
and
be in
my still attention

•

i receive patterns
from my own tongue
old ones
and failed ones
like these squashed
plums left on the sidewalk
rotten or stuck
i try to clean them
pick all each up
and fill up a compost bin
so the big trucks will take them away
to make something better

•

the sand at the beach is skittered
with trash sticks
bottle caps
dog shit
and plastic bags
and at night snowy plovers
who run in a packet
and fly real fast

•

it is now cold out
it is december
and when i am walking
i see the tents
and hope that the people
who cities dont love
have a warm something
to bug like a glove
thats a little too small

•

i hope existence
where all of the grandmas
stay here alive
they never die
so they can plain love us
how the whorl wont
encourage
respect
foster our beings
like we are ice cream
and we love them more

vi.

i offer the firemen a reverence for moons
the ones in the big truck
who came when i called
and before they would pick up
the man who had fallen
into the street
they shamed him for drinking
said
too many beers!
i think that they should go
and look at the moon
it might make them nicer
see people as people
if they go tonight
and they look at the moon
for a while

i am afraid
of writing my thoughts
there are so many
places i have fucked up
and i never want to cause people pain
with my blind spots
the size of the great lakes
aches rains
or drops
of ink on the paper

If *Book of the Other: small in comparison*, was Truong Tran's navigation through the darkest part of the forest, *Looking and Seeing* is the continuation of the map in the ongoing case study to bring one's existence to the forefront in communication with whiteness. Tran transitions his proximity to whiteness, showcasing the progression of one's positionality within his ongoing journey in self-proclamation. In this book, we gain a more intimate understanding of the intention of the other. I made this art for you not in the hopes that you will hang it on your wall but in the sense that you will hold its consciousness that you will see yourself as others see you as question as subject as metaphor as conflict that art as human is conflicted and confronted. Tran requires us to sit with his examinations, with his witnessings, his confrontations, and his consciousness. we look, but Tran reiterates "do we see?" and if seeing was the precursor to understanding, what can you do to shift your positionality in the ongoing struggle against whiteness as a threat? whiteness as inherent. whiteness as the standard. whiteness as the goal. whiteness as dominance. whiteness as foe. whiteness as illness. whiteness as dismally & unimpressively; whiteness. by taking on this joint project with Potter, Tran showcases the possibility and intimacy of engaging with whiteness without the doldrums of performance. placing brown and white together on a conversational canvas to enrich the complexity of solidarity and truth.

MIMI TEMPESTT
Author of *the delicacy of embracing spirals* (City Lights, 2023)

Truong Tran's newest book is a new kind of contraption, a language chamber that splits the infinities of Belonging and Accountability (and Rage, and Memory, and many other concepts besides) into the refracted light that is the Poem in its most beautiful and affecting shape: the form of survival. I always applaud Truong Tran's bravery in the face of this world we molded out of chingazos, vast and unruly. This book screams and bites and protects all the people who think of themselves as the smallest dot.

RAUL RUIZ
Author of *Mustard* (Drop Leaf Press, 2022)

LOOKING
and
SEEING

Cover photograph: Carolyn Ho
Cover art: Truong Tran
Cover and interior typeface: Futura, Helvetica, Georgia and Arial
Cover and interior design: Carolyn Ho

Library of Congress Cataloging-in-Publication Data

Names: Tran, Truong, 1969- Looking and seeing. | Potter, Damon, 1985-
Seeing and looking.
Title: Looking and seeing : poems, essays, fragments / Truong Tran. Seeing
and looking : poems, essays, fragments / Damon Michael Potter.
Other titles: Seeing and looking | Seeing and looking.
Description: Oakland, California : Omnidawn, 2023. | Two works bound
back-to-back and inverted; titles from separate title pages. | Summary:
"Looking And Seeing is a poetic work of equal parts yearning, regret and
righteous indignation. On these pages, what is said and what is written
renders us seen in all our complications. I wrote this book as a
singular and lifelong investigation of my being and my body as someone
brown moving through white spaces. That it now finds itself bound
together in a single volume and in proximity to the work of my friend
Damon Potter, that he is a white man and I am a brown man, and that I am
writing this into existence, means the world to me. Seeing and Looking
is a recording taken in proximity to my friend Truong Tran. In this
book, I examine who I am and who I want to be, the complications and
realities of trying to be good while also benefitting from our
oppressive past and present. I am oppressor. And also my friends die.
Someday I'll die. I witness horrible acts. I witness the moon. I
remember awful grains I've committed myself. In Seeing and Looking, I
wonder how to be respectfully dying while everyone else is also dying.
In Seeing and Looking, I witness my self"-- Provided by publisher.

Identifiers: LCCN 2023019350 | ISBN 9781632431233 (trade paperback)
Subjects: LCSH: American poetry--21st century. | Self--Poetry. |
Death--Poetry. | Autobiographical poetry, American. | LCGFT: Poetry.
Classification: LCC PS595.S43 L66 2023 | DDC 811/.6--dc23/eng/20230627
LC record available at https://lccn.loc.gov/2023019350

Published by Omnidawn Publishing, Oakland, California

www.omnidawn.com
10 9 8 7 6 5 4 3 2 1
ISBN: 978-1-63243-123-3

Poems • Essays • Fragments

LOOKING
and
SEEING

truong tran

OMNIDAWN • OAKLAND, CALIFORNIA • 2023

CONTENTS

i. breathe

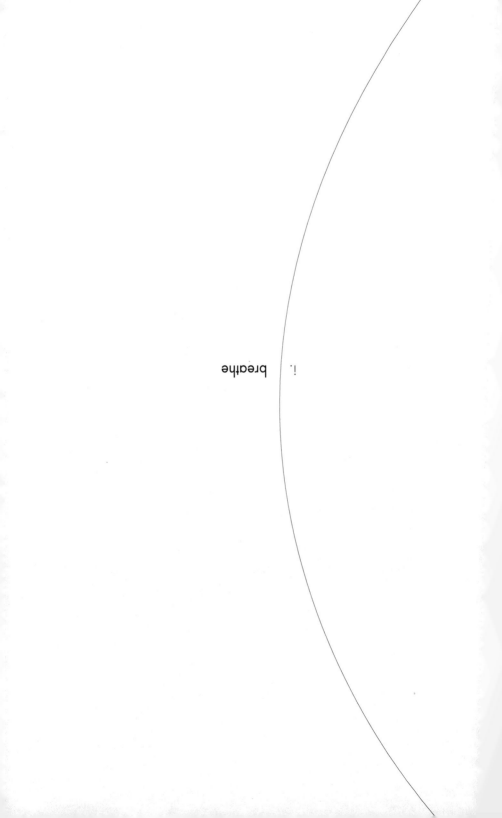

1.

some things are easier when written as poetry
when seen as metaphor when say
it shook me your words
when you declare yourself a loner
that something said about the self
can cut so deeply in the other
as to remind the other of his otherness
you wrote this to me "I am a loner"

I read the words as "leave me alone"
I cannot tell you why those words
cut the way they cut away
when I too wield this blade at will
when I say I want to be left alone
so as to live alone that is to say that I am lonely
I'm afraid of the answer to this question
but right about now I need to ask.
should I be leaving you alone.

2.

I helped a woman get up from a chair. I merely extended my
arm in passing. she took a hold and just like that. she stood up
right. she held my arm for just an instance. proud
of her feat. today just this. I held myself accountable.

3.

to be personally accountable. is simple in these times. it is after
all. the age of selfies. it is. the accountability of others. that
will cause pain. that nagging pain. runs down your back. the
friend. the colleague. the neighbor. your uncle. who chooses
not. to see. claims of complexities. it's complicated. they say.
this notion of nuance. as if to say. what you are seeing. it's not
what you're seeing. they choose to leave these at your feet.
you pick them up. you put them in your pockets. you carry
this weight. you feel the nagging pain that is your back. all
this because. you do not know. how to not be. the friend. the
colleague. the neighbor. his nephew. this is all too familiar. to
exist in these times. it is about you. no. it's really about me.

4.

(researching the fetish of masculinity or sunday morning internet
porn)

on youtube there are videos of men exacting pain. each using
the flat of a board to inflict pain upon another. the willing
participant anticipates. howls. struts about. he embraces each
assailant amassing his masculinity. the video inevitably ends
with him putting his bruised buttocks on display. on camera. this
right of passage. this badge of manhood. this thing they do.
they do on youtube. they do in life.

5.

(eulogy for the living)

a word is a breath. a line is breathing. I wake up in the
mornings to tell myself that I am not. that is to say I have been
avoiding this task. at the water's edge he called his mother.
once sharp and precise this is the line. these words are pavers
on a path towards. the sadness of living overwhelms this effort.
he left his shoes up on that bridge. I am walking to know. I
have the capacity to move. I am drinking to hydrate from this
feeling of drowning. making is a response to all that's been
taken. this writing. this breath. this breathing. this poem. I am
eating to sustain though sustenance is suspect. a death did
happen to make this happen. that is to say would I have written
this at all. this is not a departing note. he marked the spot
conveying distance. or is it proximity. he wanted to be found. I
thought I could hide in cryptic language until I got lost in cryptic
language. I am not close to him and still I know where. when.
and why. that is to say I don't like writing this. now. blunt and
bruising this is the poem now. as I know it.

6.

I went online last night. I looked for the saddest scene from
the saddest movie I could recall in that moment in the night. I
found it. I watched it. I watched it again and again and again.
I started crying. It began as tears. silence. I watched it again
and again and again. I started sobbing. I saw myself in the
reflection on the screen. I did not recognize who I had become.
I could see him but he could not see me. His cries at times
appeared to be a celebration. or was it a mourning for what
had been lost. I am writing this poem the morning after. I am
looking for something I thought I lost. I don't know what. Not
sure where. Have you seen it. or him. or some part of me. I'm
afraid of asking who are you for fear that in asking I will lose
you.

7.

(he is white and I am not)

when I fought for my rights. when I refused to accept what I
clearly understood as discrimination. when this was happening
to me. someone suggested that I just go somewhere else. to
seek employment. that someone was the same someone who
asked me to write an endorsement on his behalf some twenty
years ago. when he was an adjunct. when I was his student.
when someone brown mattered in the consideration of someone
white. when does this really matter. when my brown body in a
white room in academia serves the purpose of documentation.
representation. statistics. when diversity is used as a form of
diversion. in other words. this is when the white man claims
complexity. when the argument ends with the declaration of.
it's complicated. when conscience or the lack of is veiled
behind assertions of nuance. when the white man is saying
he deserved to be here. his language. his thinking. his way of
seeing. his belonging. he is really saying. you don't belong.

8.

it used to be that I would write to enact a desire for isolation. it was a way to say. I want to be left alone. to my thoughts. with my words. I want you to leave me alone. can't you see that I'm trying. I'm trying to write. I'm thirsty. I'm writing these words to quench my thirst. I write alone in the hopes that I would write myself into exhaustion. into sleep. I did just that. and that was when you came to me. carrying water in your mouth. you leaned into. you passed it along from mouth to mouth. our lips did not touch. this was not a kiss. a kiss would not have led me here. you woke me from sleep by quenching my thirst. this lasted but a minute. I am thirsty again. today I'm writing. it's usually to someone. I am writing something. I want to hear it read out loud. I want to see it on a page. in a book. I want to see you inside these words. where are you. I am thirsty. how are you.

9.

I worry that I come off as if I know something. as if I'm older and experienced when in fact I know little to nothing of the world into which I breathe. I don't know how I arrived at this thought. I don't know where I am going with the next. why did I laugh at that racist joke. tomorrow I'll wake to learn that I am. will always be the butt of some racist joke. the joke begins with some guy's name.

10.

my teacher's income cannot afford the intimate conversations that come with therapy and therefore I am unable to convince some stranger to write a prescription for happy on my behalf. I have no choice but to write myself through this to that.

11.

this morning I couldn't get up. get out of bed. I laid there frozen
watching that part of me that still conformed to expectations.
I watched that part of me put on his pants. gauge the body's
odor before putting on a clean shirt. I watched him brush his
teeth and wet his hair. I watched him put on socks and look
for his keys. he closed the door. he locked it from the outside.
I heard him get into a car. I heard it drive away. for hours
nothing. I'm lying here. still frozen. still waiting. and then I see
these words. he's writing as I am reading. he agrees with your
point. of what's the point. he arrives at an answer. he writes
these words to point the way home. how are you. in a few short
hours he hopes to be back in his own bed. asleep. in the hopes
that he will wake up. get out of bed.

12.

what remains.

a grown man wakes to the words of another. he eats the words as though eating for sustenance. he saves the best parts for when he knows the pangs of hunger will awaken in the night. for when he'll reach for that morsel. wrapped in a sheet of thinking wishful. he kept it tucked in a book. in a bag full of words. he will be exhausted and ready for the fade. that comes with memory to this surrender another day. living is another day dying. a grown man childlike will eat words in bed. he will write a line before closing his eyes. the line will read a note to the self. that I'm still eating. that I'm still hungry.

13.

today I became that memory from some twenty years past
when a man old enough to have been me today a stranger in
every way walked up to me today I conjured the exactness of
this memory I said what he said some twenty years past I said
it to the young man on the sidewalk with someone laughing
about something or another I said well actually I yelled too loud
too loud sssssssh. and just like that I became the memory I am
the older man in my memory I remember thinking that he was
crazy today I saw the look of this young man he looked at me
as though I was crazy I looked at him some twenty years past
I saw myself as the young man seeing myself as the crazy old
man.

14.

this time on a tuesday. in the time between this construction of
class. the world slows down. amidst the noise of traffic in the
distance. just enough to have a thought. to look out a window.
look down. look back. look in between. I am thinking of you.
the note you sent me late last night. You wrote as though
confessing a crime. of your discomfort for knowing. you do not
always know what it is that you read. and still you get excited
for the discovery. that is to say that she is black and I am asian
and you are white and this is context. I am writing to you to let
you know. I know. this is something worth knowing. between
the sum of us. without your note I couldn't arrive here. this. did
I ever tell you of that one time. I bought my roommate a danish
desk. it was locked. it didn't come with a key. it sat in his room
for over a year. one day while walking in my neighborhood.
I just happen to look down. I saw a key in a crack on the
sidewalk. I picked it up. I put it in my pocket. one day while
doing the laundry. I found that key inside my coat pocket. I
took it home. I threaded the key through a keyhole in the desk.
and just like that. the key unlocked. the drawer opened. there
was nothing inside. The drawer was filled with emptiness. my
roommate says. he keeps his belongings inside that drawer.
He keeps it locked. for when he'll need it. for when he knows.
in the same way that I will keep your note. your words. your
discomfort in not knowing. I'll keep it locked inside these words.
this drawer made of words. for when you'll need them. for
when you know.

15.

this consideration of belonging is so often connected to place/
a geographical location that allows us to identify a brother/
sister. a mother and/ or father. located inside the structure of a
house/ omniscient in assuring/ in time/ this place will become/
a home/ in a community in proximity/ to the other in a city/
town in a nation/ country this consideration of belonging
fosters yet another consideration of connectivity/ a person
belongs/ because he/ she/ they belong to/ with/ in a space
or an other for as long as my body has known its capacity to
store/ compartmentalize/ make sense of memories of the self
I have been coerced/ made/ surrendered to believe that this
is the goal/ this is the reason/ this is the objective of living/
breathing/ talking/ eating with strangers/ family/ adversaries
alike in the hopes that they/ will become/ no longer strangers/
family/ adversaries still so often these interactions between/
the self and the other are often strange/ if not estranged/ all
this in an effort to say/ I am writing this now because/ I do
not feel this sense of belonging/ I am often alone/ even in
the most crowded of spaces/ inside this urn of ash and words
sometimes/ not always/ this time this is the closest that I will
come/ to being honest so/ this consideration of belonging/
perhaps this happens in the space of words/ that you belong/
to an other's words/ that I belong inside/ your words.

16.1

discoveries.

this is the story of a man. he spent his adult life writing. poetry
he was determined. to be a poet. he learned the rhythms of
his voice. the shaping of his image. the breath of his line. the
precision of. his anger one day. the man stood in front of two
white men. one white woman owning the privilege of judging
the man. and so they smiled they. let him speak they. asked
the occasional question they. listened or so he thought they.
chose not to speak other than to say the catered lunch would
be Indian. on that day an evaluation was written. a statement
was scrawled that simply read. truong is a nice person but he is
just a poet. no name no effort to elaborate. just a sentence. not
even a period. the precision of my anger.

16.2

he carried language like bags of sand. words put on him by
passing strangers. across the desert while reading a book.
listening to people riding the bus. angry words not worth
repeating. he carried these words into his house. the poem.
words polished and adorned in a box. in the academy. the
essay back into memories. of childhood. of lording language
over his parents. he carried language and its regrets. and still
he carried them in his pockets. on his shoulders. and tucked
beneath the folds of his skin. the word debated over what was
said. and what was heard. the soft a. the hard r. words written
as commentary. truong is a nice person but he is just a poet.
he carried this sentence. until one day he found. the weight
too much to bear. was it the nice. or the but. or the just. or the
poet. or was it the inclusion of his name. that brought him to his
knees.

17.

I spoke of this with you today this is the impossible I think of it every day if only we could undo unsay I catch myself mid thought mid wish I take it back for fear that I would unlive all that we have lived the hundred ways we carry our weight how we word at nights manic conversing over coffee you said you wish between us that we could have a second language today when I went to embrace you to say goodbye I remember wishing If only I could be a little bit taller if only you could be about a foot shorter our embrace could be aplomb alas these two words are of a different time if only we existed under different again I catch myself at mid wish this symmetry of language like the curves of our backs as we reach forward to embrace we form a plum we fruit our fates your face I would never want to unsee your face.

18.

I was asked this morning how I begin writing I responded by
saying that I've not written since my last drink I have been
thirsty I went deep in the well to find this water I cupped it with
my palms "because I both want to protect you from and explore
this fucked up world with you" to bring it towards my waiting
lips what I am trying to say what I am trying to write what I am
trying to ask is simply this.

19.

always the palm before the bombing/ the ache of writing in
the middle sometimes I wake/ this is my memory of the self/
rendered in color on a television screen/ I am a child. a girl
in this memory/ acted by a former student/ who is in reality
my godson's mother/ who happens to be an actor as a child/
she died not once but twice on screen/ as a martyred hero/
communist by design/ as an orphan/ othered and defined/
that she would come all this way/ across an ocean not yet
perceived in a mother's womb/ died and again/ died to live as
herself/ a mother/ that I would see myself portrayed as dying/
living in technicolor/ a lifetime inside a time life photo in black
and white/ of a gun pointed at the head of the enemy/ the
gun the camera/ the enemy the other/ the executioner the self/
executed in living/ this photo or that/ the child once naked
crying walking in sight of american soldiers/ forever dubbed
the napalm girl/ the noise and the poise it takes to make/ this
way with words/ this calm/ my life/

20.

it seems that I am able to write in prose what I cannot say in
life that I want or am sad or wounded or still waiting and so
it seems I am writing you these words to say that I've made
something with your image I've made it as art to be hung on a
wall for others to see to react to look at you and your words/
me and my making to look inside in the hopes that they might
be moved see themselves so that you know I made this art for
you not in the hopes that you will hang it on your wall but in
the sense that you will hold its consciousness that you will see
yourself as others see you as question as subject as metaphor
as conflict that art as human is conflicted and confronted that
the art I made for you can look back out into the world that it
can see you existing in the world I have often wondered if the
subject inside the painting ever wanted to see herself as the
subject inside

21.

of being asked of the privilege tucked inside of words of
distances in language in space and consciousness the truth is
this I do not know what I'm supposed to say and still I say it as
if I know what I'm expected to say is that privilege makes it so
that one plays with words like playing with lives that metaphor
is a luxury that some of us cannot afford this is not my original
thought a student said this as a way of confronting this weight
he premised inside my pockets and still I carry it with me today
I carry this weight as if it were mine even as I write this I am
thinking of the fallacy of such a statement not from the student
who says this and means this with intent of living in the memory
of his skin he is saying what needs to be said the truth this
fallacy I am speaking of is mine to own in that I am writing
these words as metaphor I am positing one consciousness while
inferring another I am choosing to exclude you from being in
harm's way that I should think that I can probe this privilege
while asserting my own I am calling this a poem of someone's
life as if to claim this as my own as lived as living

22.

that you would ask this of me. that I would comply by building
this stage. that I would stand on this stage looking down at
my feet. that I would disrobe an article at a time. there is no
tease in this. no performance. you tell me to go further. that I
would consider what is meant by further. that I would go deeper
inside myself. reading and rereading what you had written.
"that we wanted to see the work go further in its examination
of the issues it sets out to engage–race–on a personal and
societal level. trauma around racist practices. etc. etc." perhaps
you forgot that by "work" you are referring to me. there is no
distance in language here perhaps this caught me by surprise
that you would ask this of me. that you are a white man writing
this. that I am not and still I am reading this. because you
asked. perhaps I caught you by surprise. that I would look up.
look down. that I would be the one holding this gaze. seeing
you naked on a stage. there is no want in this. just need. that
this is something still needing clarifications. that all this time you
thought that you were looking at me. that all this time. I've been
seeing. the likes of you.

23.

they. is what I have to remind me of self. to remind me of
myself. they. is what I say to remind me of other. to remind me
of my otherness. they. is what I hear to remind me of that place.
over there to remind me of my place. they. is what I write to
remind me of what's written. to remind me of how I have been
written. they. are what I look at to remind me that I am. looking
and not just to be looked at. they. is what I wield to remind me
in this fight. to remind me to fight. they. is what I hold. to remind
me in this time. to remind me in due time. they. is what I know
to remind me of them. to remind me of us.

24.

anything is possible to the extent that you hear me and I see
you. pastel perplexed by primary hues. there is no negating.
saying is staying. so let us negotiate the terms of our actions.
this knife fight is a dance of nascent neighbors.

25.

neglected and left to its ruins. I thought there was a need for weeds growing in the world. I still believe this to be true. I let it grow. I locked the gate. I turned away. I let that part of me that was enshrouded in the thorniest of language exist. thrive. I still believe this to be true. I lost the key I did not bother looking but someone did. someone found it. opened the gate and started pruning. shaping. planting the bulbs and watering the words. you say we are manic in our exchange. I came to a better understanding of that just this morning while digging through the dirt to plant this language. I paused in the middle of an image. a thought. looked up to see a garden in full bloom. you in a remote corner seeding the soil. you have been the gardener all this time. I believe this to be true.

26.

the mother is covering the child's eyes while reading the text imposed on the body. there is only one you who will know what it means to read this text. this poem she is reading. looking even in the most public of context. this seeing is private. you and I.

27.

Sometimes waking. walking to the end of the street is all I am capable of. to know I am living this time. I came to that corner I waited. I walked a few steps further. I crossed the street. I declared it a metaphor.

28.

my friend believes she's being followed. she's being hacked.
she came for a visit. she asked if she could take a shower. she
asked to sleep on my living room floor. I sent her home with a
sandwich. an apple. and a promise. of something. I don't know
what.

29.

the attic was always my favorite place. dusty memories of the
lost and found. it was where I went to find new stories. hidden
inside of old pictures. in a shoe box I found my mother. as a
young woman still looking for her look. before he came looking.
I found my father still full of pride. before he surrendered to a
fated life. I found myself in a field of dandelions. I was found in
that memory of a young man. found in his parents attic finding
himself. there are no homes with attics or photos on paper. not
in this time. there is only loss in the lost and found.

30.

I am reminded of that time I took my ball. I squeezed out the air
until it was flat. I took it out of that sandbox they call it poetry
still. I swore I would never build castles with poets. Tonight
I thought I could finally sleep. Your words arrived and I am
responding as promised. as primal. Is this a prayer if not a
poem.

31.

I came across an image by accident. a wooden vessel made by a man named Martin from Amsterdam. I was so moved by seeing this image. I wrote to Martin. I told him my name I told him I cried when I saw his work. for when I die. I wanted my ashes inside his urn.

32.

forgive me for suggesting...

I feel compelled to say I'm sorry. this is precisely why I want you to come to visit that house. to rearrange the furniture. to set fire to the trash bin filled with the refuse of their refusal. to see. to ask the question of why this is still necessary when we already know. why I want your perspective in that room. I want to see you sitting in proximity to someone like me to me. one day when your words are sitting in proximity. when you will speak to your own and I will get to listen. to think. to stand in comfort to the side. in my silence I feel compelled to say. I'm sorry for my selfish wants. for the walks that lead you through this path. for the fear that I too will fail us in our want. that I want you at my side. inside that place for all that is known and still the blind spots. and still unknown.

33.

I did not say a word today. I thought a lot. I texted a friend. I responded to emails. I went to the store and bought a soda. I paid for it with exactly eight quarters. I smiled when the guy at the counter said thank you. I lied when I wrote that's fine when it's not. I proposed an idea in no less than 1.000 words. I came with a pitch. uncertainty + adaptability + writing = existing. I thought that's not bad. not good but a start. I rode the bus without paying the fair. I didn't talk. I avoided eye contact when I saw the woman walk towards my seat. I got up. I went towards the back. I stood by the door. I got off the bus and walked a few blocks. I got in a fight with a stranger on facebook. I came home. I shopped on ebay. I bought socks from china. I wrote to a guy making urns in amsterdam. I asked him a question. could all my ashes fit in the urn. I'm waiting to see if he'll write back.

34.

my father would dismiss this as no more than his hobby
although it seemed more like an obsession. this practice of
bonsai gardening. all that time put towards this whittling away.
this pruning. this primping of the branches. my father has long
passed. his tree all but forgotten until just now. only now do I
know the meaning of his labor. this desire to put oneself into the
smallest representation of living and the self. through a lifetime
of scars and wars. my father would never claim such a thought.
but I believe my father existed as a tree. on a spoonful of dirt
contained within a potted thimble. I came to this conclusion
while reading the words of a writer who sits in a room. all six
feet five inches of him. whittling away until the entirety of his
being. sits on that thimble. beneath the shade of my father's
tree.

35.

if this poem is a window. would I be standing on the outside looking in. would I see myself sitting at a desk. writing a letter while looking out. and if this window is broken. the brick is sitting on the sidewalk. no one seems to know who when or why. from where you're standing perhaps. you can tell me what's missing. in the moment. what would be needed. to complete this thought.

36.

there is a window propped open with a stick. on a sill. there
are those who look out. and others who look in. some are
clothed. and some are naked. there is the warmth and the
wind. the weight of the frame will break the stick. the window
will shut. someone will be left out in the cold. someone will want
out from being trapped in.

37.

this sense of not belonging. I wear it like a coat. crisply ironed
and kept always. a pristine white cranberry red. an absolute
black depending on the day. the nature of the job. I wear it
as a uniform. I put it on the minute I walk into the house. I go
through the back entrance. I put on this coat to remind me
that I have never been invited. and yet I've been here for all
these years. some days the butler (I'm told that this metaphor is
dangerous in this time.) I pour water while standing next to the
table. the occasional gardener. I weed what's growing what's
dead. what's done. sometimes I teach their children. I give them
organic treats when their parents are not looking. and every
once in a while I catch a glimpse of someone I know. someone
from the neighborhood. or from back home. or someone I
met at dinner. clandestine. I see her sitting at the table I make
an effort to pour her some water. I make eye contact in that
exchange in an effort to say. I see you. I see that part of you.
they've placed and plated. in the middle of the table. my friend
speaks of this as a sense of unbelonging. the invitation. this
curation. is not inclusion. I wait until she steps away. she goes
to wash your hands. I invite her to dinner away from this house.
and back at home. we drink pimms. we eat the food of our
knowing. we arrive at belonging.

38.

some say folks. in the hopes of connecting. folks please vote
as if your life depended on it. as if my life. folks invoked as a
way of bridging the divide. as if my folks can be stand ins for
your folks. kinfolk as kindred. that is to say. folks are akin to the
pronoun of we. that is to say. we is a matter of life and death in
desperate times. there is you and there is I. making for the sum
of we. have been meeting at a coffee shop on fridays for some
weeks. the sum of our talking led some toward anguish others
anchored. that is to say someone saved my life today. that is
to say. there is more to we than you and I. we are grounded.
grieving. folks we are growing still.

ii. begin again

39.

dear you or etc.

(feel free to replace you with the pronoun of we)

not too many people can say that they left their home and their country on a boat. well ok it was actually a ship. a korean tanker to be exact. my family and I left in the hopes of finding a better life. in the case of my father. my mother would say. it was about the preservation of life. I am not writing this now out of any desire to retell my story. I've written it more times than I care to count. I've given you and yours what was expected. I am writing this now for the purpose of learning this art of irony. hold on to this knowing for the time being. know that my people have been called boat people by your people.

●

who gets to ask the person experiencing trauma and racist practices to take their "work" further into the examination of race "on a personal and societal level. trauma around racist practices. etc." in full disclosure. it was the etc. that set it off. I am asking you this in response to your response. work. who. you.

●

: the use of words to express something other than and especially the opposite of the literal meaning

: a usually humorous or sardonic literary style or form characterized by irony

: an ironic expression or utterance

•

this is a new story. I am telling this story as a joke 43 years in the making. it's taken me this long to arrive at some semblance of a punchline. how could I have known that you would come along to deliver such a pithy narrative thread. now that I have it. you will just have to wait. wait for it. wait... wait...

•

: incongruity between the actual result of a sequence of events and the normal or expected result

: an event or result marked by such incongruity

: incongruity between a situation developed in a drama and the accompanying words or actions that is understood by the audience but not by the characters in the play

— called also dramatic irony. tragic irony

•

the boat person was floating in the ocean. he was hoping that the boat passing in the night would be so kind as to pick him up. the person on that boat having decided not to pick the boat person up. went through a transformation. he became we for the purpose of responding to the boat person's ask. in

the pronoun of we perhaps as a way to show some unifying presence some collective consciousness. a collateral of sorts. he said "We all empathized with the speaker. but agreed that we wanted to see the work go further in its examination of the issues it sets out to engage–race–on a personal and societal level. trauma around racist practices. etc." when asked by the boat person how he could go further into his own trauma or the racist practices that was happening to him. the pronoun we chose not to respond for some reason or another. Without responding to the specifics of the boat person's questions. the pronoun we floated away on that boat. the boat person could hear their collective voices saying. "We want to support you in completing this project."

•

"how." asked the boat person as he floated boatless in the night as the nightboat floated further away.

•

I am learning irony so that I can write this story. not the immigrant story of my family. not the story of trauma or racist practices enacted on Brown and Black bodies. that story was written. it is being written and I will write it again and again and again. this is a particular story written to be told as a joke full of what I think is irony. a vietnamese writer labeled as a boat person by white people gets his manuscript rejected by a group of white people on account that he did not go deep enough into his account of "race–on a personal and societal level. trauma around racist practices. etc." but that's not the irony or humor of this story. wait for it... the white people are part of this literary endeavor. wait for it... they go by the name of Nightboat.

•

get it. boat people. Vietnamese people. white people. white
boat. Nightboat.

•

: a pretense of ignorance and of willingness to learn from
another assumed in order to make the other's false conceptions
conspicuous by adroit questioning

•

is this funny. have I gone further into my examination of the
work. are you laughing. Am I laughing. would you say that
this is irony. that this is ironic. and still I ask. is this funny. is this
far enough. do you get it. it's a joke. is it on you. is it on me.
are you laughing with me. are you laughing at me. should I be
laughing along. are you laughing. etc.

•

note: the definition of irony has been provided for the purpose
of reading this work in case you still think I got this all wrong.
I am prepared "to go further in its examination of the issues
it sets out to engage–race–on a personal and societal level.
trauma around racist practices. etc." the work is it. the it is I. no
need to empathize being that we are all boat people here. you
in the form of we claim it so. I was called this. and so I guess
that makes me so. perhaps you as we can give me guidance
on where to go. on second thought. forget I asked.
i think I know where not to go. thanks for the inspiration to
write the above. I rather like it in an ironic sort of way. and still
I ask. Is this funny.

irony noun
iro·ny | \ ˈī-rə-nē also ˈī(-ə)r-nē \

•

40.

I grew up catholic in the eighties. I acclaimed myself an atheist only to arrive at saying I am now an agnostic. agnosticated in writing this. it did not occur to me until just now. I never once identified as adam. I don't like apples nor am I attracted to men with too pronounced an adam's apple. I do find adam somewhat attractive. I mean wasn't that always the agenda. I am brown having gone through conversion. I have consumed the white wafer of communion. I have confirmed and have been confirmed. adam is white by all accounts. where am I going with this assessment.

41.

I don't know what to say when attempting to say. this funny
money will not do. I don't know how to say when failing to say.
I'm dying my way towards buying my urn. I don't know when
to say when wanting to say. burn my body and stash my ash
inside this book. inside this poem.

42.

now that we've stopped the exchange of metaphors. the manic ways of wading through words. there is no way to hide nor words to hide behind. no one. no wonder in the when not worded as a question. what will become of the wanderings. so that you know. I wanted a friend before findings in the forest. I wanted connection before creating. how then will we. hello. how are you. ok I'm fine our way out of dangers way. towards being strangers. ok in truth. is never ok.

43.

that coffee shop I spoke of a while back. you know. the one
I'm talking about down the street from your apartment. it
was owned and occupied by an older couple. I'm guessing
european. they spoke with an accent. I'm guessing french.
I spoke of how we met there on fridays to talk. of how our
discussions fueled my writing. I hope it fueled yours too. well
that coffee shop is closed. there is still a note left in the window.
saying thank you and goodbye. it felt appropriate reading that
note in this time. the swiftness of it. the severing. the severity. it
was not until this morning when rereading these pages. that I
thought of that coffee shop. of you. and of the things we lose.
without knowing our belongings.

44.

ok as in I'm fine ok as in there's nothing to talk about ok as in I
really don't want to say ok as in leave me alone ok as in there's
nothing left to say ok as in it's really not ok ok as in is it ok that
I leave this here ok as in I'm sorry I asked this of you ok as in if
that's what you want ok as in this is what you're asking of me
ok as in I don't agree but that's ok ok as in this ends in silence
ok as in let's keep moving ok as in I'm tired ok as in why are
we doing this ok as in what do you want me to say ok as in
eventually it would come to this ok as in I don't know what
to say ok as in we're strangers you and I ok as in this is my
burden I'll carry it til I die ok as in did you mean for that to hurt
ok as in I know how you hate that word I'm saying it anyways
ok as in I'm here ok as in I think I'm done ok as in let's not do
this anymore ok as in are we finished here

45.

if any of this should truly exist. look for it inside the memory.
inside this breath. inside the silence. inside and of this book.

46.

in a room in heated discourse. someone said I heard a soft a.
while another insisted he heard the hard r. as if the degree of
one's offense is dependent on the phonetics of the tongue. as
if the deliberation of spelling. grammar. is somehow connected
to decency or denial. as if defining the said defines the crime.
defines the person. defines this time. as if in hearing the soft
a. the hard r. in registering one's reception. the listener is
implicated. it should be noted here again. that no black persons
were present in the discourse. in the consciousness. in this
room.

47.

(for my godson Tai)

that you should find this in a book. no title attached to lead you to this finding. I want these words to be forgotten long before they are to be found. I write this to you from the past with the understanding that I will fail you to the best of my abilities. you will fall and I will not be there to catch your fall. I trust in willing that you will stand up. you will run in circles around my circle. you will bring meaning to this language in ways that escape me in this moment. I want you to know I've written this note not knowing what to say. while knowing what I feel. I found a letter in my wallet. it was a simple note written to me on the day of my graduation. it spoke of pride and love. I kept if for years. I lost that letter when I lost my wallet. finding the letter did little for my understanding of the world. losing that letter meant the world. and so it is I'm writing you this note. I'm putting it in this book. it does not matter what I say. what matters is that I lose this note and with it the world. what matters is that you've found it. I was hoping you would find it. now tell me who you are. and tell me what you're doing.

48.

(after Patrick Cassidy's Funeral March)

a composition comes along. a drum beat cues. and I am
marching into war. or is it life. or is it both.

49.

sometimes I want to write. about you. I want to say things. I want to talk. as though you are not present. I want to question. why. I want to hold you accountable. for the things you have done.
and even more so. for the things you have not done.

●

you want that I should write. about race. as long as race. is rendered as identity. you want that I should write. about race. and then you ask. why does it always have to be.

●

sometimes I want to not write. about you. I want to not say things. I want silence. as though you are present. I already know. why. I will not hold you accountable. for the things you cannot do and even less so. for the things you are still doing.

●

It's not that I want. to write. about race. as long as race. is rendered as identity. it's not that I want. to write about race. it's that you asked. and then I said. because it's always going to be.

50.

now that I'm not writing with you. I'm not writing to you. I
find myself. writing about you. it is as though. I'm writing
my thoughts. into a box. and not a book. it is as though. I'm
keeping secrets. I hide them in the hopes. that someday. you'll
find them. I find myself. writing things. that I would never.
say to you. so that it's clear. so that you know. I did not know
this. until just now. like how I thought. this would be different.
had I been. an older white man. I could have gone for walks.
talked with you. of infusing vodka. avoiding the talk. of racism.
infused. into everything. ever. exchanged. between. if you must
know. I wish you never told me. of your talks. of how he. told
you. I didn't belong. that you must know. I feel betrayed. by this
language. that binds you. to him. and I. to you. now that I'm.
writing about you. I'm writing myself. inside this box.

51.

to live is to imagine a time when I will die. I say this in the most practical of considerations. I could be walking down the street sometime next week when I am struck by a car. it could be next year while doing just this. writing a poem in bed. listening to the overture of miller's crossing. only I will not be begging for my life. I will not have a gun to my head. and I will not see it coming. or perhaps some thirty years from now when I am living full of anticipation. and suddenly I'll have this overwhelming need to make one last work of art. write one last poem to apologize to someone or another. there will always be somebody in need of an apology. so if you're listening. or if you're reading this now. and you are who I think you are. we are connecting at this moment to you and you and you and you. this is not for you. ours is a bitterness I'll keep for when to all the other you(s). I'm sorry for whatever it is that I might be guilty of. don't worry I'm not dying now or today or anytime soon for that matter. it is better to say this now than to wait. if you are reading this. if you think that this applies to you. if you are listening. I'm sorry. I say this as though. as if I know.

52.

I've said this all along. I have no choice in the matter. it is only
the illusion of choice. if you are made to feel small by being
told that you are small. if you are compared or contrasted to
someone unlike yourself like lowell or plath or some nondescript
white male up the stairs and down the hall from where you are
compared then declared that you are no comparison. if this is
happening to you and you think you have a choice between
confronting others who highlight your otherness by addressing
you by your last name. if you have a choice between this and
the countless realities of letting it go so as to slide yourself into
the next moment or day or conflict in a lifetime of conflicts. not
if but when. not when but why there is no choice in the matter
there is only the sentence. my sentence reads. I go by Truong.

53.

and just like that a bomb goes off in a room and the process of rebuilding begins anew. there will be little if any pleasantries in the weeks to come. you will know yourself in this rebuilding. you will be fearful of what you know before you claim this knowing as knowledge. you will hide sharp objects inside your poems. you will dig up old tools of mongering. hone its edges in anticipation of the war. you tell yourself you are ready to fight if provoked to fight. you invoke the teachings of your inner bully. if he calls you this. you call him that. remember words are weapons when said in the right tone. at the right time. you hit them while they're down. a word is a kick. a punch. a bullet should you need bullets. you gather. you wait. you sit in a vacuum waiting inside. and just like that a bomb explodes outside in the distance. you rush to the window. you look. and then you see...

54.

the truth is I want to write into abstraction because I want to
avoid the reality of this time. my stomach turns when talking of
this moment. the truth is abstraction is a luxury I can still afford.
when confronted by a friend. the truth is I am told that his
anguish of anti semitism is not to be conflated with my anguish
of racism. the truth is I am writing towards a future. I will not
be there in time for breakfast. the truth is. I don't think this is
working anymore. this abstraction feels like a distraction from
looking. seeing. this killing. this violence. this language of hate.
this honing of hatred. this is happening. now.

55.

the truth is there will always be thorns. slivers. cuts and pricks
when considering the skin. that language like paper will hold
our meaning. cutting deep beneath the surface.

56.

what is left is the looking back there is no going back from
where you came from the road behind is collapsing beneath
your feet the only path is the one before there is no walking run
because you must there is no mining for metaphors no breath
to pause on no rhythm no time soon even this will be a crime
in class today my student asked what are we to do you run
you hide you live you rhyme you change pronouns you make
you write fight you breathe I told my student that this was not a
response to her question this is my to do list we should all have
a to do list

57.

it's not that I would ever do it but sometimes I wonder how life would change if I knew the number to be finite and named. would I get to grading my papers tomorrow. would I learn how to drive. would I even care. would I give it all away. would I want to live on as a diamond made of my own ashes. would I stop mourning the future. anticipating the past.

58.

the united states is just one of 13 countries to have voted
against the united nations resolution condemning the death
penalty for having gay sex. no language was altered in the
transcribing of the above headline. no metaphor was used
in the processing of the above statement. no conscience was
accessed in the thinking of the above cruelty.

59.

this need to make it into being. staying awake at all hours of
the night. cutting shaping choosing. what it is you choose not to
say. this object of words and images and things and thoughts.
this need to make it by this date. at this time. to invite the
viewers to look. to see. provide them with alcohol. feed them
some cheese. stand in a corner of a room. watch your viewers
as you silently count one mississippi two mississippi three. make
it to ten mississippis and you can tell yourself that you've made
art. and you've made it this far. you are this close to dying.

60.

today when asked to price my art I gave a number thinking it
was too high a price for my wayward children. thinking that no
one could want them at such a cost. when the collector simply
said yes. when she said I want this one. and that one. when
she asked that I pack them with bubble wrap I did exactly what
was asked of me. she paid in cash she took them away. am I to
think of this as dying. is this today's sketch of actualized death.

61.

am I a masochist that I find myself reveling in that instance
the skin breaks open. the truth is. if I am bleeding. begin by
celebrating the consciousness of our living. then place your
hand on the wound. apply pressure. touch. that I should want
the process of healing. even if it does yield scars. I'll know my
right from my left. I'll know where you are. my proximity to you.
this mark. in relation to you. this map making of my body.

iii. | a work in progression

62.

that moment when your friend the tall skinny white guy asked if you have a thing for tall skinny white guys.

63.

I saw myself fumbling with language as though my tongue had fallen out of my mouth. I heard myself asking why can't you answer this question head on. I wanted to take what was asked as an invitation. an opportunity to address this elephant hiding instead. I fumbled. I tripped. I took my tongue and shoved it deep down my own throat

64.

I said it was complicated in the same way that I have become accustomed to white men saying it's complicated.

65.

when I went to embrace you that afternoon to say goodbye. it felt more like I was saying farewell. could you sense my shame in that instance in embracing. how could you have known.

66.

what I'm trying to say is this. I want to unpack what is inside
this object. this veiling of the self. this word I invoke as a way of
hiding. complicated as a container. the complications within. I
am trying to take ownership of the words found inside.

67.

desire as a complicated attempt at arriving at the truth. I can
leave this consciousness at your doorstep. leave it up to your
interpretation.

68.

how to even begin.

69.

I want to begin by saying yes I have a thing for tall skinny
white guys. this prescription of perfection. what is desirable
in the world. I am ridden with shame for having shared this
thought. in my defense. for the time being. I am going to say it's
complicated

70.

they are visible out and in my mind. just as I am invisible out
and in theirs. I want to say yours. I want to say you. but here
lies the complication. when I see you and you see me. when
desire of the other is a desire to be seen.

71.

I consider myself a sadist for the simple understanding that I can
not endure pain not in the slightest. And yet these words and all
that came before.

72.

desire of the other is a desire to subjugate from the perspective
of the subjugated. I want to imagine the white male other. this
prescriptive perception of societal perfection. he is always
the first to point out his imperfections. surrendering his being.
giving up power. I want to see this exchange as a transaction.
contractual and consensual. I have this desire to exist in a more
equitable society where I am the subject and not the subjected.

73.

you saw a version of this poem framed previously as fiction or
was it fantasy. you said you are letting us white boys off again.

74.

the tall skinny white guy is punished for crimes that are not
his own. the punishment is methodical. layered. he is made to
cry. nurtured. nursed back to a state of knowing self. I want to
believe that there is kindness and revelation and perhaps even
relevance pertaining to this time. this act in the exchange.

75.

you ask that I write what is to be true.

76.

you are the tall skinny white guy. it has always been. it will
always be you.

77.

the s/m consideration of this desire is to physically inflict pain
onto the other using my hand or a blunt instrument. the flat
of a ruler. a wooden spoon. the heft of a bath brush. the tall
skinny white guy goes to retrieve the instrument of his demise.
upon returning he hands this object to the other. he willingly
surrenders to the other's exacting infliction. as a ritualized
practice. I want to enact this as metaphor. as life. as both
experienced and endured

78.

desire is the hope of a better existence. this requires the
breaking down of a structure with the intention of rebuilding.
in case you are asking what does this have to do with my
wandering eyes. my instinctual reflex to the tall skinny white
guy. would you believe me if I said everything.

79.

it is not my place to break you down. to rebuild what's broken.
you are doing this on your own. desire on my part is the
wanting to help. in breaking down. in building up. I want to
draw you a bath infused of epsom salt.

80.

if it were only as simple as calling it lust or kink or fetish or type. one's desire to be punished and the other's to punish.

81.

that moment when you realize the tall skinny white guy is more than just your friend. what do you do. how can you say. how do you leave this knowing unsaid.

82.

desire is the want of seeing the other. his willingness to surrender as I have surrendered. the whole of my life. this concrete statement will now be made a metaphor. desire is the want of seeing and saying. someone other than yourself. other as sub. as missive.

83.

Dear D. our conversation from last night. it's taken me my whole life to arrive.

84.

I am very particular when it comes to porn. I cannot watch women or men of color in bondage in any scenario or any capacity. my preference is limited to tall skinny white guys.

85.

when making art I use the image of tall skinny white guys.
I choose to both frame and cut into these images. this
metaphorical violence exacted and enacted onto the white male
body. I was confronted by a stranger about this practice. he
said isn't that violence when you choose to be so specific.

86.

desire as infliction as sadism as masochism as the self as other
as this presentation of the tall skinny white guy as you as I as
you and I.

87.
With regards to the previously mentioned confrontation. I
said to this stranger. the act of singling out any one identity
is inevitably violent. all that is left is the distinction of the
metaphorical and the real.

88.

in response to your question. he was a white guy tall and not
that skinny.

89.

in the movie version of this poem. the captive played by a
young tony curtis says to his roman captor something to the
extent of beat me punish me but don't send me away.

90.

you asked that I say and write what I want to say. no one has asked that of me before. this writing. this saying. has always been based on needs and necessities. if this is what you ask of me. then this is what I'm asking of you.

91.

desire is the writing of this poem. it is the knowledge that my language fails my thinking in the present. the hope is this. that you would know. what is inside when I say.

92.

you ask that I write what is to be true. I have a complicated relationship to a tall skinny white guy. I want to hurt you and heal you with my own hands. I want to indict you for all the crimes committed by your kind. I want to exonerate you. none of this is of your doing. and still I see what you are doing.

93.

in the most current version of this poem I've taken away the framing of fiction or fantasy at your suggestion. the you and I inside this poem arrive at the pronoun of we.

94.

in the 2018 remake version of this movie the captive and the captor are no longer romans they are played by people like you and I. let's just say we are playing the part of ourselves in this version of the movie. the white boy is not let off by his own volition in this version of life. we are both captors and captives.

95.

if I continue to write this poem it will inevitably end in tragedy. devoid of realism. I would rather not do that if I could. this feels right. perhaps even real.

96.

Dear you. all this I'm writing. I'm saying. I'm asking. of you.

My love and thanks for all those who brought this
endeavor to its arrival.

Rusty and Laura and everyone at Omnidawn
for trusting us with this vision. And to the memory and spirit of Ken.

Mimi and Raul
for your generosity of spirit and words.

Jennifer
for your insights of knowing me.

Carolyn
for your artistic eye and keen attention to detail in all things in life.

And **Damon**
for planting that first maple that continues to grow.

Truong Tran was born in Saigon, Vietnam.

He is the author of seven previous books of poetry, including *Four Letter Words* (Apogee Press, 2008), *Book of the Other: Small in Comparison* (Kaya Press, 2021) which won the American Book Award, and *100 Words* (Omnidawn, 2021), which he coauthored with Damon Potter. Truong lives in San Francisco and teaches at Northwestern University (previously Mills College) in Oakland, California.

Looking and Seeing
by Truong Tran

Cover photograph: Carolyn Ho
Cover art: Truong Tran
Cover and interior typeface: Futura, Helvetica, Georgia and Arial
Cover and interior design: Carolyn Ho

Printed in the United States
by Books International, Dulles, Virgina
On Glatfelter 55# Cream Natures Book 440 ppi
Acid Free Archival Quality Recycled Paper

Publication of this book was made possible in part by gifts from Katherine & John
Gravendyk in honor of Hillary Gravendyk, Francesca Bell, Mary Mackey, and The New
Place Fund.

Omnidawn Publishing
Oakland, California
Staff and Volunteers, Spring 2023

Rusty Morrison, senior editor & co-publishers
Laura Joakimson, executive director and co-publisher
Rob Hendricks, poetry & fiction editor, & post-pub marketing,
Sharon Zetter, poetry editor & book designer
Jeffrey Kingman, copy editor
Liza Flum, poetry editor
Anthony Cody, poetry editor
Jason Bayani, poetry editor
Jennifer Metsker, marketing assistant
Sophia Carr, marketing assistant

Seeing and Looking
by Damon Potter

Cover photograph: Carolyn Ho
Cover art: Truong Tran
Cover and interior typeface: Futura, Helvetica, Georgia and Arial
Cover and interior design: Carolyn Ho

Printed in the United States
by Books International, Dulles, Virgina
On Glatfelter 55# Cream Natures Book 440 ppi
Acid Free Archival Quality Recycled Paper

Publication of this book was made possible in part by gifts from Katherine & John
Gravendyk in honor of Hillary Gravendyk, Francesca Bell, Mary Mackey, and The New
Place Fund.

Omnidawn Publishing
Oakland, California
Staff and Volunteers, Spring 2023

Rusty Morrison, senior editor & co-publishers
Laura Joakimson, executive director and co-publisher
Rob Hendricks, poetry & fiction editor, & post-pub marketing,
Sharon Zetter, poetry editor & book designer
Jeffrey Kingman, copy editor
Liza Flum, poetry editor
Anthony Cody, poetry editor
Jason Bayani, poetry editor
Jennifer Metsker, marketing assistant
Sophia Carr, marketing assistant

Damon Potter lives and works in San Francisco.

Potter's poems have previously been published in *Elderly and Mirage #4/Period[ical]*. He is the author of *100 Words* (Omnidawn, 2021), which he coauthored with Truong Tran.

Thank You

Mimi, Raul, Carolyn, Jennifer, Laura, Rusty, Patrick, Estivaly, and Truong.

i want to un
claim
all of the times
ive ever said
they
that othering vein
damon within me

vii.